LEVEL 2

W9-BAF-963

Thomas Edison

Barbara Kramer

NATIONAL GEOGRAPHIC

Washington, D.C.

For Terry —B. K.

The publisher and author gratefully acknowledge the expert review of this book by
Paul Israel, director and general editor, Thomas A. Edison Papers, Rutgers University.

Book design by YAY! Design
Trade paperback ISBN: 978-1-4263-1476-6
Reinforced library binding ISBN: 978-1-4263-1477-3

Cover, (portrait) Library of Congress Prints & Photographs Division; (lightbulb), CreativeNature.nl/SS; 1, Corbis; 2, SSPL/Hulton
Archive Creative/Getty Images; 4, Library of Congress Prints & Photographs Division; 5, Mike Groll/AP Images; 6, Alan Copson/Jon
Arnold Images/SuperStock; 7, The Granger Collection, NYC—All rights reserved; 9, Bettmann/Corbis; 10 (UP), Bettmann/Corbis; 10
(LO), Library of Congress Prints & Photographs Division; 11 (UP), Ryan McVay/Photodisc/Getty Images; 11 (CTR), Library of Congress
Prints & Photographs Division; 11 (LO), Library of Congress Prints & Photographs Division; 12, U.S. Dept. of the Interior, National Park
Service, Thomas Edison National Historical Park; 13, The Granger Collection, NYC—All rights reserved; 14, The Granger Collection,
NYC—All rights reserved; 15, U.S. Dept. of the Interior, National Park Service, Thomas Edison National Historical Park; 16, Library of
Congress Prints & Photographs Division; 18 (UPLE), Corbis; 18 (UP CTR), U.S. Dept. of the Interior, National Park Service, Thomas Edi-
son National Historical Park; 18 (UPRT), U.S. Dept. of the Interior, National Park Service, Thomas Edison National Historical Park; 18
(LO), The Granger Collection, NYC—All rights reserved; 18-19 (Background), MaxyM/SS; 19 (UP), Flickr Open/Getty Images; 19 (CTR
LE), H. Armstrong Roberts/Corbis; 19 (CTR RT), Dorling Kindersley/Getty Images; 19 (LO), Library of Congress Prints & Photographs
Division; 20 (UP), Aksenova Natalya/SS; 20 (LO), Library of Congress Prints & Photographs Division; 21, PoodlesRock/Corbis; 22,
Education Images/UIG/Getty Images; 23, Library of Congress Prints & Photographs Division; 24, Corbis; 25 (UP), Library of Congress
Prints & Photographs Division; 25 (LO), Joseph Sohm/Visions of America/Corbis; 26, Lebrecht Music & Arts/Corbis; 27 (LO), Michael
D Brown/SS; 27 (UP), Bettmann/Corbis; 28, Corbis; 29, Corbis; 30 (UP), Corbis; 30 (CTR), Ryan McVay/Photodisc/Getty Images; 30
(LO), Corbis; 31 (UP), Library of Congress Prints & Photographs Division; 31 (CTR RT), Library of Congress Prints & Photographs Divi-
sion; 31 (CTR LE), Dan Saelinger/Corbis; 31 (LO), Bettmann/Corbis; 32 (UPLE), curve/the Agency Collection/Getty Images; 32 (UPRT),
Wendell Metzen/Photolibrary RM/Getty Images; 32 (CTR LE), Susan Steinkamp/Corbis; 32 (CTR RT), The Granger Collection, NYC—All
rights reserved; 32 (LOLE), Library of Congress Prints & Photographs Division; 32 (LORT), Ryan McVay/Photodisc/Getty Images; top
border of pages, SoleilC/SS; vocabulary boxes, Studio Barcelona/SS

National Geographic supports K–12 educators with ELA Common Core Resources.
Visit natgeoed.org/commoncore for more information.

Printed in the United States of America
14/WOR/1

Table of Contents

A Great Inventor

Have you ever watched a movie or listened to a recording of music? Have you ever turned on a light? If so, you can thank one man: Thomas Edison! He made all these things possible with his inventions (in-VEN-shuns).

In His Own Words

"Nothing is impossible. We merely don't yet know how to do it."

Thomas Edison worked day and night, with little rest, to make his inventions perfect.

Early Learning

Thomas was born in Milan, Ohio, on February 11, 1847.

The Edison family home in Milan, Ohio

When he was seven, his family moved to Port Huron (HUR-on), Michigan. In school, Thomas daydreamed. His teacher said he could not learn. So, after only three months of school, his mother decided to teach him at home.

Learning from his mother was fun. She taught Thomas to read.

When he was ten, he got a book of science experiments (ek-SPER-uh-ments). He tried every one of them in a lab he built in the family's basement.

Four-year-old Thomas Edison

Words to Know

EXPERIMENT: A test done to discover or learn about something

LAB: Short for laboratory, a room or building used for science experiments

A Working Boy

Thomas was only 12 when he got his first job. He sold newspapers and snacks to people on a train.

At the train station, Thomas liked to hang out with the telegraph operators. They sent messages to other train stations. Watching them, Thomas knew what he wanted to do next. He would learn to be a telegraph operator.

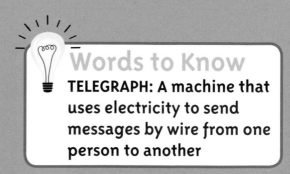

Words to Know

TELEGRAPH: A machine that uses electricity to send messages by wire from one person to another

Young Thomas in his railway uniform

That's a Fact! When Thomas was working as a newsboy, he built his own telegraph. He and a friend practiced sending messages back and forth from their homes.

In His Time

When Thomas was a boy in the 1850s, many things were different from how they are now.

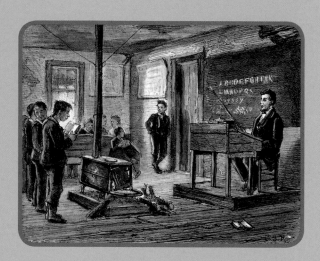

School

Children often went to school only in winter. They worked on farms or in mines or factories the rest of the time. Many of them did not go to school beyond sixth grade.

Transportation

People traveled by horse and wagon or steamboat. The railroad was just becoming popular.

Communication

The telegraph was the fastest way to send messages. Alexander Graham Bell had not yet invented the telephone.

Toys

Boys played leapfrog and marbles. Girls played hopscotch. Indoors, they all enjoyed the Snake Game. It was a lot like Chutes and Ladders.

U.S. Events

Thomas was 13 years old when Abraham Lincoln was elected president in 1860.

First Inventions

Thomas began work as a telegraph operator when he was 16. He liked to work nights. During the day, he worked on his inventions.

He got his first patent in 1869. It was for a vote-counting machine to be used by legislators (LEJ-is-LAY-turs) in making laws. But no one wanted to buy it.

Thomas's vote-counting machine

Words to Know

PATENT: An official paper that says no one else can make or sell an inventor's work

LEGISLATORS: A group of people who have the power to make and change laws

That's a Fact! Thomas hired people from all over the world to work with him. They helped turn his ideas and sketches, or drawings, into new inventions.

T. A. EDISON.
Electric-Lamp.

No. 223,898.

Patented Jan. 27, 1880.

Fig 1.

Fig 2.

Fig 3.

Inventor
Thomas A. Edison

Lemuel W. Serrell
atty

Thomas did not give up. He worked on other inventions, such as ways to make the telegraph work better.

Always Working

Thomas was so busy working, he did not have time to think about getting married. Then in 1871, when he was 24, he met 16-year-old Mary Stilwell. He liked her right away, and they were married a few months later on Christmas Day.

In His Own Words

"There is no substitute for hard work."

Thomas and Mary had three children. Thomas loved his family, but he did not spend much time with them. He was always working.

In 1876, he opened a lab in Menlo (MEN-loh) Park, New Jersey. There he often worked all day and into the night. When he got tired, he took a nap on a lab table.

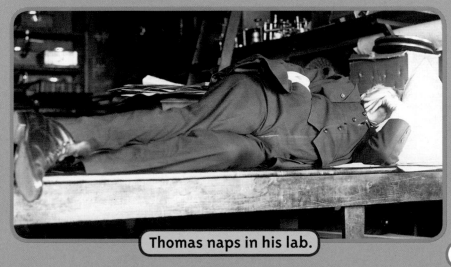

Thomas naps in his lab.

The Wizard

Thomas thought his phonograph could be used to record books for the blind.

One of Thomas's early inventions was the phonograph, which recorded sound and played it back.

Thomas had an idea for a new machine. Finally, he was ready to test it. He shouted the poem "Mary Had a Little Lamb" into the machine. The machine played it back! Thomas and his workers stayed up all night having fun with the new machine. They called it the phonograph (FOH-nuh-graf).

This invention made Thomas famous. People called him "The Wizard of Menlo Park."

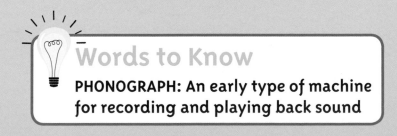

Words to Know

PHONOGRAPH: An early type of machine for recording and playing back sound

7 Awesome Facts

2

Thomas nicknamed his first two children "Dot" and "Dash," the short and long sounds used by telegraph operators.

1

When Thomas was 15, he saved the life of a 3-year-old boy, pulling him from the path of a rolling railroad car.

3

When Thomas and his helpers worked late, they had dinner at midnight. They ate and told stories. Then everyone went back to work.

4

On the train where he sold newspapers as a boy, Thomas also wrote and printed his own newspaper, *The Weekly Herald*. It was the first newspaper printed on a moving train.

5

Of all of Thomas's inventions, the phonograph was his favorite. He called it his "baby."

6

It was Thomas's idea to answer the telephone by saying "hello." Alexander Graham Bell wanted to use the word "ahoy."

7

Thomas and his lab staff filled more than 3,000 notebooks with ideas and sketches for his inventions.

Lights On!

Thomas was soon working on his next idea. He wanted to make an electric light. Electricity had been around for a long time, but no one knew how to light a house with it. Instead, people used candles or oil or gas lamps.

Gas lamp

In His Own Words

"I can never find the thing that does the job best until I find the ones that don't."

One of the filaments that Thomas tested

To make an electric light, Thomas needed something small that could be heated inside a bulb to make it glow. This small thing was called the filament (FIL-uh-ment). Thomas and his workers tried hundreds of things. The best answer was a thin piece of bamboo.

In His Own Words

"Genius is one percent inspiration and ninety-nine percent perspiration."

Thomas had a working lightbulb, but he was not done yet. He made lamps and switches to turn the lamps off and on. He built power stations to make electricity. He used underground wires to carry that power to homes. It took him four years to invent everything he needed to light homes with electricity.

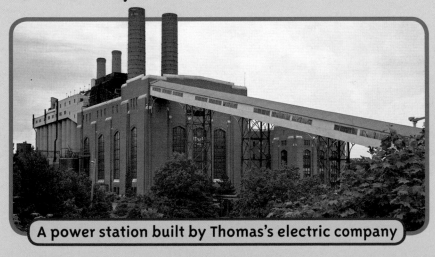

A power station built by Thomas's electric company

Changes

In 1884, Mary Edison died. Thomas was sad and lonely. Then in 1885, he met Mina Miller, and they married a year later.

That's a Fact!

Thomas had six children—a daughter and two sons with his first wife, Mary, and another daughter and two more sons with his second wife, Mina.

Thomas and his wife, Mina, enjoy an automobile ride.

Inside Thomas's lab

Thomas's new home in New Jersey

They moved into a 23-room house in West Orange, New Jersey. There Thomas built a new lab much larger than the one in Menlo Park.

Always Inventing

Thomas went back to work on his phonograph. He had invented it to record people speaking. Now he began making records so people could listen to music on it. He also invented a movie camera and a machine to show short movies.

One of many styles of phonograph Thomas built. This one is from 1905.

1847	1854	1862	1869	1871
Born on February 11 in Milan, Ohio	Moved to Michigan	Began work as a telegraph operator	Got his first patent	Married Mary Stilwell on December 25

Thomas began losing his hearing when he was a child. He said it helped him be a better inventor because he wasn't distracted by noises around him while he was working.

Thomas's machine for viewing movies

Thomas worked on many other inventions, too. In all, he got 1,093 patents. That was more than any other inventor until the year 2000.

1876	1877	1879	1886	1931
Opened his lab in Menlo Park, New Jersey	Invented the phonograph	Created a bulb that provided hours of light	Married Mina Miller on February 24	Died on October 18

A Great Honor

Thomas began experimenting when he was a boy. More than 70 years later, he was still inventing! He worked until a few months before his death on October 18, 1931. He was 84 years old.

Thomas Edison (right) with President Herbert Hoover

People across the country were sad. At 10 p.m. on October 21, 1931, they turned off their lights for one minute. It was a way to thank the man who had brought electricity into their homes and changed their lives. Thomas Edison made the world a better, easier place to live. We still use his inventions every day.

In His Own Words

"I think work is the world's greatest fun."

Be a Quiz Whiz!

See how many Edison questions you can get right! Answers are at the bottom of page 31.

1

When Edison was a boy, people _____.

A. Watched television
B. Talked on the telephone
C. Used candles and oil or gas lamps to light their homes
D. Traveled by plane

2

Before the telephone was invented, the fastest way to send messages was by _____.

A. The U.S. Postal Service
B. Email
C. Telegraph
D. Steamboat

Edison's first patent was for _____.
A. A telegraph
B. A phonograph
C. A movie camera
D. A vote-counting machine

3

able Commissioner of Patents:
etitioner *Thomas A. Edison*
ark in the State of New Jersey
PATENT may be granted to him

Edison had _____ children.
A. Three
B. Four
C. Five
D. Six

Edison invented _____.
A. A phonograph
B. Ways to make the telegraph work better
C. A movie camera
D. All of the above

Edison got _____ patents.
A. About 3,000
B. More than 1,000
C. About 500
D. More than 2,000

People honored Edison a few days after his death by _____.
A. Building a large statue of him
B. Playing music on their phonographs
C. Turning off their lights
D. Flying American flags

EXPERIMENT: A test done to discover or learn about something

LAB: Short for laboratory, a room or building used for science experiments

LEGISLATORS: A group of people who have the power to make and change laws

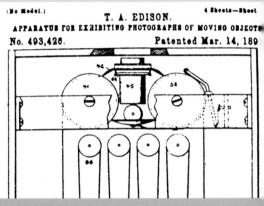

(No Model.)
4 Sheets—Sheet

T. A. EDISON.
APPARATUS FOR EXHIBITING PHOTOGRAPHS OF MOVING OBJECTS
No. 493,426.
Patented Mar. 14, 189

PATENT: An official paper that says no one else can make or sell an inventor's work

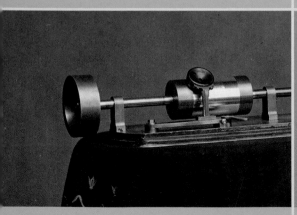

PHONOGRAPH: An early type of machine for recording and playing back sound

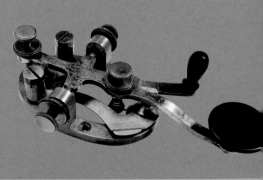

TELEGRAPH: A machine that uses electricity to send messages by wire from one person to another